W9-ASY-750

Marie Curie

Courageous Pioneer in the Study of Radioactivity

Beverley Birch

BLACKBIRCH PRESS, INC.

WOODBRIDGE, CONNECTICUT

Published by Blackbirch Press, Inc.
260 Amity Road
Woodbridge, CT 06525
web site: http://www.blackbirch.com
e-mail: staff@blackbirch.com

First published in Great Britain as *Scientists Who Have Changed the World* by Exley Publications Ltd., Chalk Hill, Watford, 1992.

10 9 8 7 6 5 4 3 2 1

Photo Credits:
Corbis Images: Cover, 20-1, 24; British Nuclear Fuels: 6, 34 (all), 61; Central Electricity Generating Board: 60; E.T. Archive: 11; Exley Picture Library: Stefan Baluk 4, 5, 7 (below), 8 (both), 9, 13, 14, 16 (top), 19, 23, 25, 27, 31, 36 (both), 40, 42 (both), 44, 49, 51, 54 (both), Wojciech Broniarek 7 (top), 38, 39, 56 (both), 57 (all); GeoScience Features Picture Library: 35; Imperial War Museum: 55; National Radiation Board: 47 (both); Ann Ronan Picture Library: 29 (both); Solvay et Cie, Brussels: 58.
Map drawn by Geoffrey Pleasance; paintings on cover and pages 33 and 53 by Borin Van Loon.

The Publishers thank Curtis Brown of London for their kind permission to quote extracts from Eve Curie's biography of her mother Madame Curie; and William Collins, Sons & Co. Ltd. of London for their kind permission to quote extracts from Robert Reid's biography of Marie Curie.

Printed in China

Library of Congress Cataloging-in-Publication Data

Birch, Beverly.
    Marie Curie : courageous pioneer in the study of radioactivity / by Beverly Birch — 1st U.S. ed.
        p. cm.—(Giants of science)
    Includes index.
    Summary: Presents the life and accomplishments of the Polish-born chemist, discussing her methods of scientific research, discovery of radium, and its use as a treatment for cancer.
    ISBN 1-56711-333-8 (hardcover : alk. paper)
    1. Curie, Marie, 1867-1934—Juvenile literature. 2. Chemists—Poland—Biography—Juvenile literature. [1. Curie, Marie, 1867-1934. 2. Chemists. 3. Women—Biography] I. Title. II. Series.
QD22.C8 B57 2000   00-008806
540'.92—dc21   CIP
                                                                    AC

Contents

A Radiant Glow

On a cold winter's night in Paris in 1902, two people stood in the dark, icy dampness of a shed. Dozens of rays of light, like glimmering "glowworms," hovered around them. Their beautiful glow held the promise of unimagined knowledge.

The moment was a rare time of absolute peace. The two people who watched the blue, glowing crystals were Marie and Pierre Curie, the brilliant young scientists who had recently discovered the element radium.

Now they peered into the tiny glass containers on the makeshift tables and shelves in the shed. The glimmering liquids and crystals seemed suspended in the darkness.

Each tiny, luminous container had taken months of painstaking work. Years later, Marie would write of how the soft glow of the radium filled her with "new emotion and delight."

Marie and Pierre stood, silently, linked by the understanding that they had opened a vast new field of knowledge—the science of radioactivity.

Opposite and below:
Marie and Pierre Curie in their shed laboratory in Paris.

5

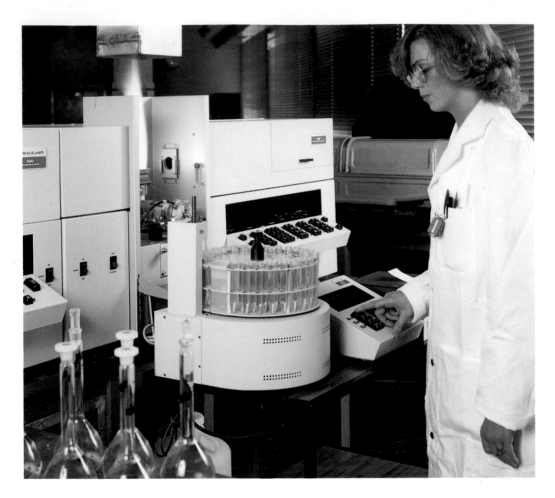

A woman scientist at work on an experiment in a modern laboratory.

The New Radioactivity

Today, scientists know what radioactivity is, how to use it, and how to make it. Nuclear power stations and submarines run on this energy. With it, industries as varied as papermaking and metal rolling control the quality of their products. Radioactivity is also vital to the improvement of crops and livestock, the tracing of pollution in rivers, and the testing of steel and concrete structures beneath the oceans. In hospitals, it is used to sterilize equipment and to diagnose and treat disease—including cancer.

At the turn of the century, radioactivity was a mystery. Scientists only knew that a metal called uranium gave off strange and powerful, invisible rays. But what it was exactly was a puzzle.

Young Marie Curie decided to explore the mystery behind uranium. She gathered together all the different materials that could give off these rays. Then she set off on a determined course into unknown territory. In doing this, Marie Curie discovered radium, an element more than a million times more radioactive than the uranium scientists already knew about.

Marie's exploration of radioactivity accomplished much more than the young scientist could have ever anticipated. The discovery of radium revealed answers to science's most fundamental mystery—the atom. After her discovery of radium, scientists began to better understand the atom, which is the basic building block of all things.

Above: *16 Freta Street, Warsaw, in Poland where Marya Sklodowska, later Marie Curie, was born.*

Childhood in Poland

On one of the cobblestoned streets of Warsaw, near the the old city walls and not far from the swirling waters of the Vistula River, there is a simple plaque next to the door of a house. The plaque reads that on November 7, 1867, Marya Sklodowska—later known as Marie Curie—was born. To her family, she was known as "Manya." Her sisters—six-year-old Sofia, three-year old Bronya, and eighteen-month old Hela—awaited Marya's birth with noisy impatience. Four-year-old Joseph took his role as her only brother seriously. Their mother was principal of a girls' boarding school, and the family lived in a few small rooms on the second floor.

Boarding school pupils' voices filled the air with chatter. Impatient young feet pounded up and down the staircases and clattered on the

Below: *This plaque commemorates Marie's birth on November 7, 1867.*

*Wladislaw Sklodowskvi,
Marie's father.*

Marie's mother was seriously ill with tuberculosis when this photo of her was taken.

floorboards above them. This was the kind of atmosphere in which the family lived.

Still it was a loving and happy family. As she grew up, Marie developed close friendships with her brother and sisters that lasted throughout her life. In fact, much of what is known about Marie comes from the letters she wrote to her brother and sisters over the years.

Marie's childhood was also a time when she first developed a love of learning. The Sklodowskas constantly exposed their children to culture and knowledge. They taught their children to use their minds in order to become useful citizens. This aim was deeply rooted in all their children. Marie's father, in particular, was an unusual, but very well-educated man. He was a quiet, soft-spoken person, who had a precise mind. He not only spoke Polish and Russian, but he also spoke French, German, Greek, and Latin. He translated some classic literature of these languages into Polish so that his children could enjoy the same literature he loved.

One day, four-year-old Marie stood on her tiptoes in front of a polished glass case in her father's study. Inside the case was a collection of tubes and bottles. Small dishes, a scale, tiny pieces of rock, and a mysterious machine rested inside the case.

"What are they?" Marie asked her father.

"Physics apparatus," her father told her. That was the young girl's first exposure to the tools of science.

By the age of five, Marie could read well. She read everything and anything she could including stories, poetry, and history. When she grew a little older—even though she couldn't understand most of it—Marie buried herself in textbooks and technical papers that she borrowed from her father's library.

Tragedy in the Family

Since Marie's birth, her mother had suffered from tuberculosis, an infectious disease of the lungs. When Marie was six years old, her mother's illness grew worse. Doing what he could, Marie's father sent his wife away for a year's rest and treatment at an expensive sanitorium in France.

This only raised false hopes. When she returned, Marie's mother only looked more frail and exhausted. Her disease was no better. The children began to fear the blood-stained handkerchiefs that their mother used when she coughed.

Then some school pupils at the school fell ill. The doctors said it was typhus, a serious bacterial disease that causes a high fever. Bronya and Sofia caught the fever, and for weeks their bodies burned with it. Slowly, Bronya grew better, but

Marie's brother and sisters, from left to right: Sofia, Hela, Marya (Marie), Joseph, and Bronya.

Sofia never recovered. On a cold Wednesday in January 1876, Sofia died. She was only thirteen. Two years later, when Marie was ten, her mother finally died of tuberculosis.

School Days

Despite the loss of both her sister and mother, Marie remained successful in school. Her teachers remembered her as an unusually intelligent child who was at least two years ahead of her classmates. She had a powerful memory and an ability to absorb large amounts of information. They also remembered Marie as a shy person, who was unwilling to push herself into the spotlight, except when she was driven by the desire to find something out. At those times, her dogged persistence overcame all obstacles.

At the end of the nineteenth century, Poland was governed by other countries. For over 100 years, it had been divided into separate areas that were ruled by Austria, Prussia, and Russia. In central Poland, where Marie lived, the King of Poland—Alexander II—was actually the czar of Russia.

The Polish people constantly dreamed of overthrowing their Russian conquerors so they could regain control of their homeland. Each time they organized a rebellion, the Polish people were beaten down. The punishment for uprisings was severe. Rebels were deported from the country, and the leaders of the rebellion were executed.

During Marie's early childhood, the Russians introduced new rules that were designed to keep the Polish people under Russian control. The Russian leaders tried to destroy the Polish language and religion. Russian officials were placed in all the most important positions in the country. Any Polish people who held important jobs were removed from their positions. Teachers were not

A painting of Warsaw in late 1800s by Bernardo Bellotto.

allowed to speak Polish, or to teach their pupils Polish history or culture.

By contrast, Marie's education was rich and varied. Every Saturday evening the family gathered by the light of an oil lamp in their father's study. He would read poetry, stories, and history to them. Sometimes he translated the great books as he was reading them aloud! This was how Marie first heard *David Copperfield* by Charles Dickens.

In 1883, when she was fifteen, Marie received a gold medal from her secondary school. Even so, the future looked bleak. Women in Poland could not go on to higher education after they had finished secondary school studies because they had not been taught the subjects needed for entrance to a Polish university or technical school.

Because he was a boy, and had been taught the proper subjects, Joseph decided to study to become a doctor. The girls—Marie, Bronya, and Hela—had only one choice. If they wanted to continue learning, the three sisters would have to go to a university in another country.

But they wondered how this could ever happen. They knew their father would retire soon. Then there would be only his small pension to support the entire family. Passports, train tickets, food, and accommodations were all costly. They could never afford to go away to school. The sisters decided they must earn a living in Poland as best they could.

A Year in the Country

Marie's studies and final exams had drained her energies. She also battled an inner sadness, a result of losing her mother five years before.

Marie's father knew something must be done to restore her spirits. He decided to send her away to stay with relatives in the country. "Rest," he told her. "Enjoy yourself. Come back refreshed."

Marie left for the countryside. There was nothing she had to do from one end of the day to the other. She could play games, pick wild strawberries, swim, or read lighthearted novels. She wrote to a school friend, "We swing a lot, swinging ourselves hard and high; we go fishing with torches for shrimps....Sometimes I laugh all by myself, and I contemplate my state of total stupidity with genuine satisfaction."

Marie began to love the changing seasons of the countryside with its varied plant and animal life. In later life, when the stresses of life threatened to break her, Marie always returned to the countryside to find the peace she had always felt there.

The year in the country came to an end. Marie, now sixteen, returned to Warsaw. She and her

Opposite: *Marie's father, with his daughters, from left to right: Marie, Bronya, and Hela.*

Marie (standing) and Bronya when they both had jobs as governesses, looking after the children of wealthy families.

sisters set their minds to finding some way to earn a living.

It was hardly surprising that the sisters' thoughts turned to teaching—the profession they knew well from their parents They began to give lessons, for a small fee, to the children of Warsaw families.

"The Floating University"

It was at this time that Marie joined "The Floating University," the name used for a group of young men and women in Warsaw who were determined to learn the things that were forbidden to them. Marie's generation of bright young people had a fierce passion to change their country's future and seize control from the Russians. They planned to start by educating themselves as best they could—and at any cost. While one of their members kept watch for curious policemen, groups of enthusiastic men and women met in secret to listen to lectures, to discuss ideas, and to exchange pamphlets and books. The young scholars wanted to learn all the new ideas emerging throughout Europe. Each member knew that, if anyone was caught, it would mean prison for all of them. Yet "The Floating University" thrived. Under the influence of this group, Marie began to yearn for a real university.

Marie and Bronya made an important decision. They would go to another country to continue studying. Both Germany and Russia were ruled out as possibilities—both places were governed by Russia. Instead, they would go to France. The two sisters felt they would find the freedom they needed in Paris.

Deciding to go to Paris was one thing. Getting there was another. The sisters earned very little by teaching. Marie proposed a plan. First, both she and Bronya would work to save enough money to send Bronya to Paris. Then, when Bronya was settled, Bronya would help Marie to save the money for the journey to Paris.

Marie made a second, vital decision. Although it meant leaving Warsaw and her family and friends, she decided to work as a governess in the country. The pay would be better, so she would be able to save more money. That way, both sisters would get to the university in Paris much faster!

On January 1, 1886, Marie left for her job as a governess. The memory of the misery she felt that day stayed with her until the end of her life. Ahead of her lay a strange job and a strange family—for an unknown length of time. Lonely and frightened by the gigantic step she was taking, Marie persevered, knowing it was all ultimately worth it.

The new job was in Szczuki, 60 miles (100 km) north of Warsaw. She found it was not at all like the beautiful countryside she already knew and loved. Sugar beet fields surrounded the town. Marie's bedroom looked out onto the red brick buildings of a smoke-belching sugar factory. All around were the unchanging lines of sugar beet fields. Nearby was a village where the peasants and sugar factory workers lived in small huts.

A School on the Beet Farm

Marie's employer managed a sugar beet estate, and he was also part owner of the sugar factory. He and his family lived in a large, vine-covered house set amid rambling gardens, orchards, barns, and cattle sheds. Here Marie settled in to teach the manager's daughters, ten-year-old Andzia, and eighteen-year-old Bronka, who was Marie's age. For seven hours a day, she instructed the daughters. For another hour each day, she gave lessons to a workman's son to help prepare him for school.

"I have a lively memory of that sympathetic atmosphere of social and intellectual comradeship [at the 'floating university'.] The means of action were poor and the results obtained could not be very considerable; and yet I persist in believing that the ideas that then guided us are the only ones which can lead to sure social progress. We cannot hope to build a better world without improving the individual. Towards this end, each of us must work toward his own highest development, accepting at the same time his share of responsibility in the general life of humanity—our particular duty being to help those to whom we feel we can be most useful."

Marie Curie, in a letter dated 1924

Above left: *Marie studied at the Museum of Industry and Agriculture on the second floor of this Warsaw building.*

Above right: *The country home in Szczuki, Poland, where Marie was governess for three years.*

One day Marie met some peasant children on one of the muddy village roads. These children could neither read nor write. They did not go to school at all. Even though she knew teaching them would be against the law, Marie decided they must be taught: "It is their right. It is what our country needs."

Bronka was enthusiastic and wanted to help. Marie's employers agreed. The two girls set up a little school in Marie's room in the family house. Gradually the children learned to read.

Marie also began another important task. In the long winter evenings, when her other duties were finally over for the day, Marie began to educate herself in preparation for going to the university. In her spacious, quiet room, warmed by a gigantic porcelain stove, she read books about every subject she could find—literature, history, sociology, and science. Marie was most fascinated by physics and by her father's favorite subject, mathematics. If she couldn't find enough time during the evenings, Marie would make time by getting up at six o'clock in the morning.

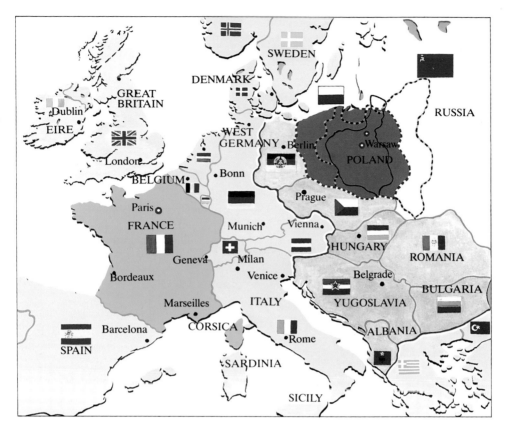

Bronya Goes to Paris

By 1885, the two sisters had reached their first goal. They had saved enough money to send Bronya to Paris to study medicine. Marie resigned herself to a long wait. The days and months passed. Marie felt lonely—in fact her homesickness often overwhelmed her. She even began to believe that she might never reach her goal of going to Paris. The dream faded, grew bright, and faded again many times.

"Think of it," she wrote to her brother in October of 1888. "I am learning chemistry from a book. You can imagine how little I get out of that, but what can I do, as I have no place to make experiments or do practical work?"

In 1867, when Marie was born, Poland was divided between Russia, Austria, and Prussia. The black line shows the Russian area. The blue-black dotted line shows the Republic of Poland following World War I. The red dotted line shows the Polish borders after World War II.

17

Three long years passed, and Marie's job at Szczuki came to an end. She returned to teaching jobs in Warsaw where an unexpected possibility opened up. One of her many cousins, Joseph Boguski, was the director of the Museum of Industry and Agriculture. This official-sounding name hid one of Poland's secret schools. Inside, there was a small science laboratory that had all the equipment Marie needed. Her cousin gave Marie permission to use the laboratory for experiments.

On Sundays and on free evenings, Marie taught herself how to use the equipment and to perform simple, scientific experiments. She taught herself how to use the apparatus, how to perform simple experiments, how to handle minute amounts of substances and liquids, and how to measure, weigh, heat, cool, and mix them. She observed the action of magnets and conducted experiments using the delicate glass tubes, flasks, and funnels. Years later she wrote about these early experiences, "From time to time a little unhoped-for success could come to encourage me, and at other times I sank into despair because of the accidents or failures due to my inexperience. But on the whole, even though I learned...that progress is neither rapid nor easy, I developed my taste for experimental research during these early trials."

In the spring of 1890, Marie received a long-awaited letter from Bronya. Her sister was firmly settled in Paris and was going to marry a fellow medical student. She had passed all of her exams, and only her final exam was left. The time was right for Marie to start her university studies. Bronya could offer her younger sister a home in Paris. She urged Marie to make final preparations.

At the end of the following year, Marie finally boarded the Paris-bound train. She was nearly twenty-four years old. To keep her living expenses

This drawing shows Marie at a meeting of Polish students in 1892.

low, she followed Bronya's advice. Marie packed her mattress, blankets, sheets, towels, her few clothes, shoes, and some hats. Her father, now elderly, stood on the platform as she boarded the train.

"I won't be long," she said to her father. "I'll get my degree, and then I'll be back." She was certain she would return soon because her goal was to graduate from the university in Paris and return at once to teach science and mathematics in Poland. As her train slowly steamed out of Warsaw, she was beginning a journey that would take her more than 800 miles (1400 km) across Europe. She was on the threshold of a new life that would bring her notice throughout the world. The personal sacrifice that fame would bring to Marie was that she would never live in Poland again.

This painting by Jean Beraud shows a street scene in Paris around 1891, when Marie arrived to attend school.

The Sorbonne

Paris was freedom. Marie could breathe it in the air. Even the murmur of people scurrying along the great boulevards was wonderful to her.

Here people spoke French—their own language! They read books of their own choice! In the crowded cafes and open-air bookstalls around the university, the hum of conversation seemed to her a vast cauldron in which momentous ideas and new philosophies melted into one another.

Each day Marie climbed to the upper deck of the horse-drawn bus and rode from her sister's home in the northern suburbs of Paris to the university of the Sorbonne.

When she first saw the university, Marie stood outside for a long time. How many times she had imagined this moment! She, Marya Sklodowska from Poland, was at the Sorbonne, a place that had been a seat of learning for nearly 800 years!

With some 12,000 other students, Marie now had the right to enter the lecture rooms and use the libraries. There was even a place for her in the laboratories of science. Memories of the years of lonely struggle in Poland fell away. She could see only the future.

But Marie encountered a problem. She could not understand a word of the lectures! In Poland, Marie's French had always seemed quite fluent—

fluent enough, at any rate, enough for her to read widely in the language. Now Marie was listening to lectures on physics, mathematics, and chemistry that were spoken rapidly in French. It was quite another matter.

Despite all her reading in Szczuki and Warsaw, Marie was years behind the French students who were starting their science courses at the Sorbonne. There were vast gaps in her knowledge.

Marie steeled herself against disappointment. The years of preparation had trained her for one thing—not to be defeated. She needed to learn French, to catch up, and to fill in the gaps in her essential knowledge. And she needed to do it quickly! These were the tasks she needed to accomplish. Marie was utterly determined to succeed. She began to spend all her time at the Sorbonne, returning to her sister's home only in the evening. Bronya and her husband, Casimir, were now qualified doctors. They welcomed Marie into their home. The friendship between the two sisters, which had sustained them through all the years of waiting and planning in Poland, was now stronger than ever. With Casimir, Bronya's husband, Marie struck up a bond of friendship and mutual respect that lasted all their lives.

Nevertheless, it was not long before the two-hour ride to and from the Sorbonne wore Marie down. And the end of each day, she was very tired and she had little time left to study. Marie, Bronya, and Casimir talked over a possible solution to the long commute. Marie felt she should take a room closer to the Sorbonne, in the Latin Quarter, within walking distance to laboratories, libraries, and lecture rooms. She knew the added expense of rent would drain her savings. Still, she was certain this was what she needed to do. By March of 1892, Marie had found a room in the Latin Quarter.

Life in a Garret

During her years at the Sorbonne, Marie lived in a succession of tiny rooms that were barely furnished and cheap. They provided her with a place to sleep and study, and that was all she wanted. Like so many of her fellow students, she had just enough money to pay her rent and to buy food and fuel so she could stay warm. Sometimes, when it got especially cold, she had to choose between fuel and food because she didn't have enough money for both.

Still, Marie was able to live for very little. In her small rooms near the Sorbonne, she was able to settle down to her routine of constant studying. She studied in the libraries until they closed at 10 o'clock at night. Then, she returned in the dark to her room to read by oil lamp until she fell asleep, totally exhausted. She walked everywhere, because the horse-bus cost money. Sometimes Marie lived for days eating only bread, butter, and tea. But she was always in her place in the front row of lectures making careful, detailed, rapid notes. The growing fascination with sciences that had gripped her in Poland now overtook her completely. She was filled with wonder by the many mysteries she learned of in the natural world.

This photo was taken while Marie was studying for her first degree at the Sorbonne.

Marie's Degrees

As Marie's first exams drew near, her whole life seemed to hang in the balance. All the years of sacrifice and hard work would culminate in these tests.

She took her first exam in July 1893, when she was twenty-five, only eighteen months after her arrival in Paris. When the results were announced, Marie was the top student!

Somehow, Marie had mastered both French and physics, and emerged ahead of all her peers. She was

This painting by Henri-Gaston Darien shows a street market in the Latin Quarter of Paris where Marie found a tiny, attic room.

unmistakably a student of exceptional, extraordinary qualities. Marie had decided not to be satisfied with just one degree. She had decided to take a second degree in mathematics the year following. Unexpectedly, she received a scholarship from Poland, which was given to students who wished to study abroad. It provided enough money for her to live in Paris for another fifteen months!

In the summer of 1894, within just one year, Marie passed the exams for a degree in mathematics with distinction, finishing second in her class.

Meeting Pierre Curie

The year 1894 had an even greater importance for Marie. Early in the year, she had met Pierre Curie at the home of a mutual Polish friend. She wrote of this moment, "When I came in, Pierre Curie was standing in the window recess near a door leading to the balcony....I was struck by the expression of his clear gaze....His rather slow, reflective words, his simplicity, and his smile, at once grave and young, inspired confidence."

So began one of the great partnerships of science. They talked. Marie, at first shyly, but then with growing confidence, asked Pierre questions about his scientific work. She sought his advice about some problems of her own.

Pierre was astonished by her broad understanding of scientific matters. She had such a lively interest, and her enthusiasm was infectious. Their conversation became more animated. He already knew from their mutual friends that she had fought to come to Paris and that she was self-educated, yet had emerged first in the physics exam. And she seemed to share his own fascination with science. She had the same drive to discover the unchanging rules that govern the physical world. Like him, Marie constantly expanded her base of knowledge.

Their meeting was the beginning of a friendship that would lead to love and a unique partnership that would bring them worldwide recognition. Pierre set about trying to persuade Marie to remain in Paris, to marry him, and to begin scientific work together.

As each day passed, Marie felt a growing bond with Pierre. He was a scientist already recognized by many of distinguished colleagues for his and original work. He was a gentle, quiet person who also had a generous nature. But he was French, and to stay with him would mean living in France and leaving her beloved Poland and her family for good. It seemed an act of betrayal.

Pierre saw that Marie could not bear the thought of leaving Poland behind for good. He offered instead to live and work in Poland with her. Marie

When he met Marie in 1894, Pierre Curie was thirty-five and already a distinguished scientist and Chief of Laboratories at the School of Physics and Chemistry of the City of Paris.

knew that in Poland, Pierre would not be able to do the work he loved or to live the life he wished. It would be too costly a sacrifice, and he would never be happy.

She wrestled with her own difficult choice: Poland and her family, or Pierre and a scientific partnership. For a whole year she hesitated.

In the end, Marie chose Pierre. On July 26, 1895, when Marie was twenty-seven years old, they were married. Marya Sklodowska from Warsaw became Madame Marie Curie of Paris.

The First Years of Marriage

Marie and Pierre had an idyllic honeymoon. Their only preoccupation was to roam the French countryside on their new bicycles, a wedding gift from a relative.

In Pierre, Marie had found a kindred spirit who also loved the countryside. Together they observed flowers, butterflies, frogs, and birds, they watched the pattern of the seasons and the cycle of plants and wildlife. Often, in the first years of their marriage, they would put their bicycles on a train and head for the countryside to explore its woods and fields.

By October 1895, Marie and Pierre had settled into a small apartment in Paris and had resumed their scientific work. These were busy, happy years. They enjoyed their work, their shared ambitions, and each other. They became so close that they learned to think together. They believed they were better scientists as partners than they would ever have been alone.

Marie was learning a great deal from Pierre's years of experience and knowledge. He was also a fine teacher. Marie was given permission to work alongside her husband in the School of Physics and Chemistry in Paris. There, Pierre taught his

students and at the same time continued with his important research on the structure and growth of crystals. Marie was just beginning her first piece of scientific research.

Pierre and Marie with their bicycles outside 109 Boulevard Kellermann, Paris, the house they moved to in 1900.

In September of their third year of marriage, Irene, their first child was born. Marie combined the role of research scientist in the laboratory with the role of wife and mother at home. It was a busy time. Within the space of just a few months Marie had produced both her first child and published her first scientific report on the magnetic properties of steel.

Doctor of Science

Marie's next objective was to start working on a doctorate. For this, she needed to find a subject for research that would break new ground in science.

She was already breaking new ground merely by undertaking this research—for no woman in the whole of Europe had ever completed a doctorate.

Marie's search for a subject began. She started to read reports of the latest experiments by scientists all over the world. One report, published in 1896, particularly caught her attention. It was by a French scientist, Henri Becquerel. Like many of the scientists at the time, Becquerel had been investigating X rays. They had been discovered in 1895 by Wilhelm Roentgen, a German scientist. X rays were a kind of invisible light that could pass right through materials like paper, wood, and metal.

Scientists had also discovered that X rays could pass right through the human body. They knew that photographic film becomes dark if it is exposed to any kind of light. They also knew that the more light the film gets, the darker it becomes. When they put photographic film on one side of a person's body and an X-ray machine on the other, the X rays passed through the body and made an image of the shape of the body on the film. The flesh was darker and the bones were lighter, because more of the rays passed through the flesh and less passed through the bones. Within days of this discovery, X rays had been used to find a bullet in a human leg.

Henri Becquerel was one of many scientists working on how X rays could be used. He knew that some chemicals glowed when X rays shone on them. He was trying to determine if other chemicals would send out X rays if a strong light, like sunlight, shone on them.

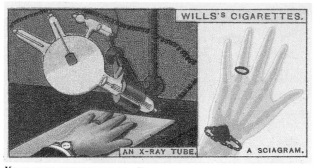

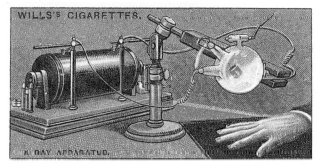

These two early cigarette cards show the popularity of scientific inventions.

X-RAY APPARATUS POWERED BY A RUHMKORFF COIL, FROM THE "FAMOUS INVENTIONS" AND "DO YOU KNOW?" SERIES OF CIGARETTE CARDS.

One day, Becquerel took a piece of photographic film and wrapped it in several layers of black paper to ensure that no visible light could darken the film. He put a metal sheet on top of the wrapped film and sprinkled it with a chemical. Then Becquerel put the film, the metal sheet, and the chemical out in the bright sunlight for a few hours. He developed the film to see if the chemical had sent out any rays and darkened the film. He did the same test with many different chemicals. The only one that had darkened the film was uranium.

One day when there was no sun, Becquerel put his sandwich of film, metal, and uranium in a drawer to wait for the next sunny day. By some strange stroke of fate, Becquerel took the film out a few days later and decided to develop it anyway. Unbelievably, the film had the dark shape of the uranium on it. No sunlight could possibly have reached the uranium, causing it to send out X rays.

Becquerel concluded that the uranium was giving out some kind of ray all by itself. These rays were strong enough to pass through the metal sheet and the black paper and reach the photographic film, just like X rays. But from other tests he did, he realized they were not the same thing at all!

Becquerel had actually discovered radioactivity. At the time, all he knew was that it was some kind of miraculously powerful ray, quite invisible to the eye and also unknown to the world.

Becquerel had his report published. But no one had yet taken up the challenge to find out what these rays were and where they had come from— not even Becquerel himself. As Marie read Becquerel's paper, she became more and more fascinated by the possibilities and by all the questions there were to answer!

Work on Radioactivity Begins

Marie had found her research subject. She was given a tiny room, used partly as a storeroom, at the School of Physics and Chemistry. Marie's first step was to find a way of measuring how strong the mysterious Becquerel rays were—the rays given out by uranium. Marie had the perfect machine to do this. It was an electrometer, which had been invented by her husband Pierre and his brother Jacques. An electrometer could measure electrical currents in air, no matter how tiny they were.

Becquerel had already shown that uranium rays caused an electrical current to flow through the air. Marie decided she would measure the strength of the rays by measuring the strength of the electrical current that they caused in the air. She obtained as many samples of metals and minerals as she could, and then she tested them all.

Przywiązać pracownie naukowe, które Pasteur nazwał "świętemi przybytkami ludzkości" — utalisiać zadanie tym, co pracują dla nauki, — otoczał opieką młodzież pragnącą wiedzy, aby pozyskiwać pracowników przyszłości, — stwarzał warunki w którychby wrodzone a cenne zdolności mogły się uświadamiać i posłużać służbie ideału, jakto prowadzić społeczeństwo drogą rozwoju potęgi, tak duchowej jak materyalnej.

Marya Skłodowska Curie

Within days, she had her first result. She found that the strength of the rays depended only on the amount of uranium in the samples: The more uranium there was, the stronger the rays. The strength of the rays was not changed by whether the substance she was testing was wet, dry, hot, or cold. Only the amount of uranium in it was important.

Investigating Radioactivity

Uranium is a chemical element. Chemical elements are the most basic materials or substances from which all things are made. At the time that Marie began her work on uranium rays, scientists knew of about 83 elements (today there are about 113 known elements).

Marie knew that uranium gave off the rays. The next question she asked was: Do any other elements give off the same kind of rays?

She tested all the chemical elements. Marie had her second important result: One other element,

This is part of a letter from Marie to her sister, Bronya. It reads: "...to create conditions in which...precious talents may be realized and devoted to the service of ideals...this is the way to lead society along the path of developing its power, both spiritual and material."

named thorium, gave out rays like those of uranium. Tested by her electrometer, they seemed to be just as strong.

Obviously, it was no longer enough to call these rays "uranium rays." A more general name had to be found. Marie began to use the word "radioactivity," a term still in use today.

Radioactivity in Pitchblende

Marie had answered the basic question that most researchers would have asked: Which substances give off these strange rays? From her research she concluded that only two elements did so—uranium and thorium.

Marie needed to decide what to explore next. Her instincts as a researcher were crucial. She wanted to expand her research, so she set about obtaining samples of all the available kinds of natural materials—minerals, rocks, sand—and she tested them all with her electrometer.

If her first results had been correct, only the samples that contained some uranium or thorium would have been radioactive. If the samples did not contain uranium or thorium, then they should not have been radioactive. Marie's analysis of all the samples showed this to be correct. Next she turned her attention to the radioactive samples.

She measured the radioactivity of each of the radioactive samples. Then came the totally unexpected, dramatic result. The samples with uranium and thorium in them gave off rays that were much stronger than could be caused by the amount of uranium or thorium. When Marie tested a mineral called pitchblende, it was four times more radioactive than chemicals she had tested that contained the same amount of uranium!

Marie did the experiment at least twenty times. Each time, the result was the same. Pitchblende

Opposite: *Marie's shed in the Rue Lhomond in Paris, where she worked with highly radioactive radium.*

It was Marie's discoveries about radiation that led to a completely new area of science: nuclear physics. The top picture shows the structure of a simple helium atom. The middle picture shows how radiation forms when an atom disintegrates. The bottom picture shows the resistance various materials have to different sorts of radiation.

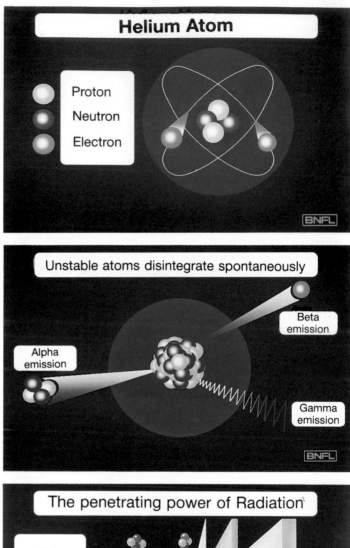

Helium Atom

Proton

Neutron

Electron

BNFL

Unstable atoms disintegrate spontaneously

Beta emission

Alpha emission

Gamma emission

BNFL

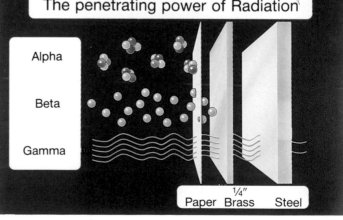

The penetrating power of Radiation

Alpha

Beta

Gamma

¼"
Paper Brass Steel

A piece of pitchblende ore, from which radium can be extracted.

was more radioactive. And what was more, the strength of the radiation was extraordinary! Where on Earth did it come from?

There could be only one explanation. There must be something else in pitchblende that was much more radioactive than uranium and thorium. Marie concluded it must be present in a minute quantity because no one had ever noticed it before. She had already tested every one of the elements that scientists already knew about. Could she have found a new element? If there really was a new element, and if it was an element with extraordinary radioactivity, then it was a discovery of great significance for the world.

On the Track of Radium

For Marie, this was a time when her work was a supreme effort of faith in her own knowledge and judgment. She had no doubt that she was pursuing a new, powerfully radioactive element. But other scientists doubted it. They were sure she had simply made a mistake in her measurements.

Above and right:
The shed where Marie produced a tenth of a gram of radium from pitchblende.

Marie knew she had made no mistakes, but she had to prove it. She had to find the unknown substance and had to show it to everyone else.

Pierre had been watching Marie's efforts with excitement. In the early summer of 1898, he decided to join Marie in her search for the unknown element.

They would look for it in pitchblende ore. Marie and Pierre already knew which elements were in pitchblende. If they separated all these elements, only the new element would remain.

In fact, Marie and Pierre had discovered not one, but two new elements. By July of 1898, they were able to confirm the existence of the first element, which they named polonium, after Poland. But all the evidence pointed to another element that was still hidden. By the end of 1898, Marie and Pierre were absolutely certain of the second element, and they named it radium. Polonium never had the same importance as radium, for it was radium's powerful radioactivity that had tremendous applications for scientists of the twentieth century.

Because Marie and Pierre had determined that radium must be present in the pitchblende in very tiny amounts, they knew they would need large amounts of pitchblende in order to extract enough of it to prove its existence. They also needed a source for pitchblende. In the end, a factory in Austria that extracted uranium from pitchblende let the Curies have the pitchblende waste.

The next problem for the couple was finding a work space that could hold several tons of ore. Marie's little storeroom would never do! The Curies had no money to buy or rent a work space, but they managed to persuade the principal of the School of Physics to let them use an old abandoned shed in the school yard. It was lit by a small skylight, and it had a leaky roof and a beaten earth

> "It is true that the discovery of radium was made in precarious conditions: the shed which sheltered it seems clouded in the charms of legend. But this romantic element was not an advantage: it wore out our strength and delayed our accomplishment. With better means, the first five years of our work might have been reduced two, and their tension lessened."
>
> Pierre Curie

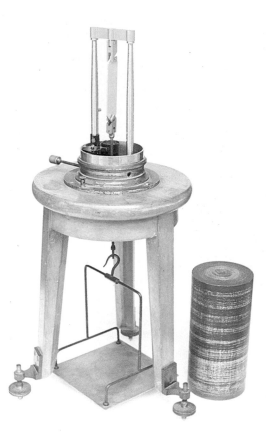

floor. In the summer, Marie and Pierre suffocated with heat. In the winter, they froze. The only advantage was that they could use the yard for some of the work, enabling the wind to blow away any poisonous fumes. For equipment, the Curies had some old pine tables, some furnaces and burners, and Pierre's electrometer.

Extracting Radium from Pitchblende

The process of finding radium was tedious. First, Marie and Pierre took a sample of pitchblende and sifted it to remove any impurities. Next, they ground up the pitchblende and boiled it with soda to separate the solids from the liquid. Then they

The original piezoelectric quartz plate used by Marie to measure radioactivity.

discarded the liquid and dissolved the solid material in acid. To do this, the solution had to be treated with different chemicals in order to separate and discard the elements they did not want. Each time they removed an element, Pierre used his electrometer to measure what was left. As the portion they worked with got smaller, its radioactivity increased. The radioactivity of the pure radium was going to be enormous!

The two scientists were at the laboratory constantly, patiently reducing each sample to a minute amount of radium. The stench of chemicals filled the shed and yard. Sometimes the wind blew iron and coal dust into the purified radium products, and Marie and Pierre had to start again.

Sackful after sackful was patiently reduced to a thimbleful of radium. Marie lifted and poured great cauldrons of fuming liquids. Sometimes, she stirred the cauldron for hours with an iron bar that was almost as big as she was. They started the process of extracting pure radium from pitchblende in 1899. It took them four years of hard work to reach their desired amount. By the time they had, they were in a state of near exhaustion.

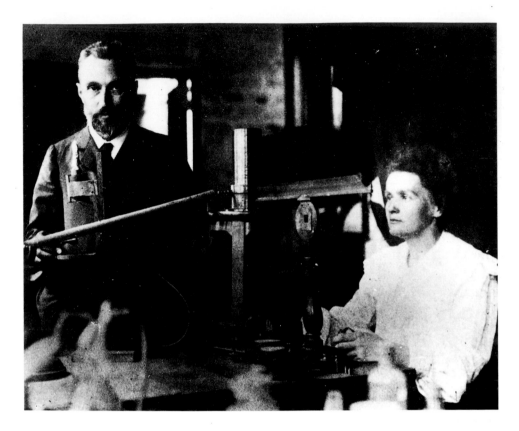

Pierre worked constantly at Marie's side during the years of her most tiring research.

Victory!

In 1902, when she was thirty-five, Marie had refined enough radium to prove its existence. She had prepared a tenth of a gram of pure radium.

Even as Marie continued with the work on purifying radium, Pierre had been studying and analyzing it. He discovered a number of very important things—among them the fact that other substances placed near radium actually became radioactive themselves. This is what is called "induced radioactivity."

During this period of exhausting work, Marie and Pierre also managed to produce a document of tremendous scientific significance. It was a summary of all the work and knowledge about radioactive substances at that time.

The science of radioactivity was now developing so fast that Marie and Pierre realized they needed other people to help them. Scientists collected around the Curies, developing their work in other areas, even before radium had been purified.

As their baby daughter, Irene, grew up, Pierre's father cared for her. In the evening, Marie would return home to the tasks of a parenting— bathing, feeding, and playing with Irene, and reading her stories until she fell asleep.

Sometimes, when the baby was finally asleep and the evening's household duties were over, the Curies would return to the laboratory. There, they would stand in the dark and look at the soft glow of their radium.

The Structure of Matter

At the turn of the century, scientists believed that they understood the structure of matter. They knew that all materials in the world are formed from chemical elements, and they thought that all elements were made up of building blocks that they called atoms. As far as they knew, the atom was the smallest piece of matter.

Marie theorized that radioactivity was not caused by something acting on a substance from outside. Instead, she theorized that radioactivity was caused by something going on inside the substance's atoms. Marie reasoned that there were minute particles agitating within the atom.

Marie never personally investigated this idea any further, but other scientists did. The discovery of radium and Marie's idea about the source of radioactivity were crucial to their discoveries about the nature of matter.

The course by which scientists reached their revolutionary knowledge was extraordinarily rapid. Even as Marie worked on purifying radium,

A page from one of Marie's meticulously kept science notebooks.

others were exploring its rays and answering basic scientific questions. What happened if you put a magnet near its rays? Did the rays affect air, other gases, solid substances, or liquids? How powerful was the heat given off by radium? Scientists learned, too, that radium made any substance near it become radioactive.

By the end of 1899, research in Germany, Austria, and France produced a sudden burst of simultaneous discovery. In France, Pierre had realized that there were two kinds of radium rays.

Work on the Atom

In Canada, a scientist named Ernest Rutherford was reading about the work of the Curies, Becquerel, and others, and adding their results to his own.

One of his experiments with uranium rays had already produced results that matched Pierre's with radium. Rutherford also discovered there were two kinds of rays. He named them alpha and beta rays. He found that when he blew air across a radioactive substance, radioactive gas was formed. He named it an emanation. Any substance that came into contact with emanations in turn became radioactive.

Rutherford was later joined in his work by an English scientist named Frederick Soddy. Together, the scientists realized that when a substance gave out radiation, its atoms were breaking up. Alpha and beta rays were actually particles of the atom shooting out as it disintegrated.

As their work continued, the two scientists were able to build up a clearer picture of the atom's structure. By 1911, Rutherford had developed a picture very similar to the one we have today. Modern science was now beginning to understand how to release and harness the enormous energy stored within a minute atom.

Rutherford and Soddy's discoveries occurred because young Marie Curie had added her discovery of radium to the scientific effort. Radium was more than a million times more radioactive than uranium. Marie's discovery of radium actually launched the start of the nuclear age.

These early workers—particularly Rutherford and Becquerel—owed much gratitude to Marie. Much of their work had been unsuccessful or disappointingly slow until she had sent them powerful samples of radium to use in their experiments.

"The Curies could have made a fortune if they had patented their process for producing radium but, poor as they were, they did not wish to take personal advantage of their discovery. They revealed their secrets to the world in the interests of humanity, and a method was devised for treating cancer patients with radium."

Norman Wymer, from
The Inventors Book

Radium as a Miracle Cure

As early as 1900, radium had revealed another great secret. Two German scientists found that the substance had significant effects on the human body.

Pierre Curie and Becquerel made similar discoveries, and both had tested the effect of radium on human skin. Pierre had strapped a sample of impure radium to his arm for ten hours. The skin became red, as though it had been burned. After several days, it developed scabs and then a wound. When the skin finally healed, fifty-two days later, there was still a scar. Marie had also carried a tiny amount of radium in a sealed glass tube inside a metal container. She had similar burns.

Marie and Pierre, with Henri Becquerel, received the Nobel Prize for Physics as a result of their research into radioactivity.

By 1903, Pierre had collaborated with two French doctors in testing the effects of radium on diseased animals. Amazingly, the radium had destroyed the diseased cells. Could it cure abnormal growths, such

as cancer? Further tests suggested that radium could be used to treat these growths.

The miracles that radium could perform seemed unending. With these tests, a new possibility emerged: a cure for cancer victims. French doctors made the first successful treatments of diseased people, using tubes of radium emanation supplied by Marie and Pierre. The new techniques of cancer treatment became known as Curietherapy.

It was clear that radium would be needed on a very large scale to supply cancer therapy. Factories were required. And so a new industry was born.

The Nobel Prize

Meanwhile, Marie prepared her thesis for her doctoral examination. It was ready by June 25, 1903. The subject was a comprehensive summary of radioactivity, a subject that had already generated great interest in the scientific community. Much had happened since she had first chosen to study Becquerel's strange rays!

The university examiners interrogated her closely, watched by a large audience of scientists, friends, and members of Marie's and Pierre's families. Marie answered their questions with certainty. Her grasp of the subject of radioactivity was immense. It surpassed that of all the others in the room, including her examiners. She had been the motivating force behind the avalanche of knowledge that she so clearly laid before them. They awarded her a doctoral degree "with great distinction." Marie was the first woman in Europe ever to receive one.

Rutherford visited them on the evening they celebrated Marie's degree. Pierre did his usual party trick: he pulled a small tube of radium from his pocket and allowed it to glow softly in the dark for the wonderment of his guests. Even though the

"It might even be thought that radium could become very dangerous in criminal hands, and here the question can be raised whether mankind benefits from knowing the secrets of Nature, whether it is ready to profit from it or whether this knowledge will ot be harmful for it....I am one of those who believe with Nobel that mankind will derive more good than harm from the new discoveries."

Pierre Curie, Nobel Lecture, June 6, 1905

tubes glow was slight, it shone like a beacon to Marie's success. But Rutherford saw how the ends of Pierre's fingers were red and sore, as though burned. None of the people in the room, however, recognized that radium could be permanently destructive to the body.

In December, Marie and Pierre won the most important international scientific recognition, the Nobel Prize. Jointly with Becquerel—who had first discovered the miracle rays—Marie and Pierre were awarded the Nobel Prize for Physics.

Radiation Sickness

The Curies were not well enough to travel to Sweden to receive the prize and give the Nobel Lecture on their work. Radium, the miracle cure, was beginning to exact a crippling toll on its discoverers. Early on, Pierre had written to a friend that Marie was "always tired, without being exactly ill." An overwhelming, constant fatigue had overtaken them. Over the four years of purifying radium, Marie had lost fourteen pounds. For some time, Pierre had been suffering from what the doctors called "rheumatism," bouts of pain in his legs that were so bad that he had to stay in bed for days. At times his hands were too pained to write properly, and he had difficulty dressing himself.

Scientists now know that air made radioactive by radioactive substances causes severe breathing disorders among workers who do not protect themselves properly. These emanations drifted freely around the Curie's laboratory. We also know that radiation from gamma rays causes serious damage to the bone marrow where our bodies manufacture blood. Many cancerous diseases are caused by these gamma rays. By 1903, all the worst symptoms of radiation sickness were already present in Marie and Pierre.

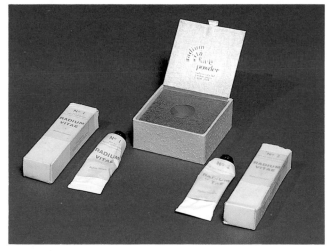

Above: *These "sparklets" for making soda water contained radon gas in the early 1900s. Who knows what it did to the insides of the people who drank it.*

Left: *Radium Vita face powder from the 1920s. Women who used this were greatly increasing their risk of developing cancer.*

The Price of Fame

Marie Curie was now famous internationally. Everyone had heard of the discoveries of the formerly obscure Polish woman. The story of her mammoth effort in the grim shed in Paris captured the imagination of people throughout Europe and America. Marie was a woman who represented the qualities of determination, energy, and excellence—at a time when few women excelled in science. Marie had proven herself to be an exceptional scientist.

A Cure for Cancer

What also captured the public imagination was the possibility in the future of a cancer cure. Because it had already helped many people, it was Marie's radium that appeared to be the "wonder cure." The world longed to see her and thank her.

This intense wish to thank Marie had, as Marie herself described it, "all the effects of a disaster" for the Curies. They were quiet, private people who wanted to get on with their work and enjoy their family and friends. Within days of winning the Nobel Prize, this was no longer possible.

The Curies began to live a life under siege, unable to move for fear of the next intrusion into their lives. "Never have we been less at peace," Pierre wrote. "There are days when we have hardly any time to breathe."

Yet throughout it all, they continued to be unswervingly generous with information about radium and the process for separating it from pitchblende. They believed that knowledge should be given freely and as rapidly as possible for the benefit of science and humanity. Working from the detailed techniques that the Curies described, whole industries were set up in Europe and America. Ironically, these industries would make vast sums of money for the already-wealthy men who founded them.

Despite constant interruptions, Marie and Pierre struggled to continued their work. The year 1904 was particularly exhausting because Marie was pregnant again. She was very ill this time. Bronya came from Poland to help her sister and was shocked by Marie's frail condition. The continual sense of ill health—which Marie and Pierre still did

....

"If our discovery has a commercial future, that is an accident by which we must not profit. And radium is going to be of use in treating disease.... It seems impossible to take advantage of that."

Marie Curie and Pierre Curie discussing whether to patent radium, from "Madame Curie" by Eve Curie

....

not link with their work—took a heavy toll. So did the effects of fame.

In December 1904, when Marie was thirty-seven, Eve, a second daughter, was born. Eve was healthy, and her antics began to breathe new life into the tired woman. Marie began to feel lighter and freer than she had for some time. The period of rest she took after having the baby renewed Marie's energies.

At almost the same time as Eve's birth, the Sorbonne created a position for Pierre. Marie was made his laboratory chief. For the first time since she had started her scientific work, Marie would be getting a salary! Now they could move out of the shed into a proper laboratory at the Sorbonne.

Marie divided her time between working at the laboratory and teaching two days a week at a girls' school near Versailles. She had begun this work in 1900 because the Curies needed the money. But with her characteristic commitment, she had

In 1900, Marie Curie was appointed physics lecturer at a girls' school in Sevres, near Paris. Marie, is shown here, with the graduation class of 1904.

introduced revolutionary changes, and had begun to teach practical science to the young girls. They would work with Marie not just from books, but with their hands.

Pierre's rheumatism continued to plague him. The bouts of pain were so intense that sometimes he moaned through the night, as Marie watched over him anxiously.

The Dreadful Year

At Easter in 1906, the Curies planned a short vacation in the country. The weather was warm, and Pierre and Marie relaxed with their two children. Surrounded by the early growth of spring, Pierre felt better. Eve, now fourteen months old, kept them laughing as she tottered on the muddy paths trying to catch butterflies.

After the short break, the family returned to Paris. The weather turned cold and wet. One Thursday afternoon in April, Pierre set off for a working lunch with university colleagues. After lunch, Pierre shook hands with everyone, put up his umbrella, and walked out into a driving rain.

In the middle of a downpour, Pierre tried to cross a busy road, crowded with carts, trams, and cars. In all the confusion, he was crushed beneath the heavy wheels of a horse-drawn wagon. Within seconds, he was dead.

When Marie heard the news, she became white-faced, and silent. In the book she later wrote about her mother, Eve tells how Marie went out into the wet garden and sat. She supposedly put her elbows on her knees, her head on her hands, as though waiting for Pierre, the companion who would never return.

Only those close to Marie knew how lonely she felt without Pierre. Yet there were decisions to be made. Eve and Irene needed her, and Marie knew

"It is impossible for me to describe the meaning and depth of this turning point in my life, as a result of the loss of him who was my closest companion and friend. Crushed by the blow, I am unable to think of the future. And yet, I could not forget what my husband sometimes said that even without him I should work on.

Marie Curie

Marie with her two daughters, Irene and Eve. The photograph was taken shortly after Pierre's death.

she needed to continue to give them a warm, loving home. She also needed to make up for the loss of the girls' father, provide an income for them, and ensure their education.

The university wrestled with the questions of how to help and who should fill Pierre's vacant professorship. It became clear that there was only one scientist capable of doing the work that Marie and Pierre had begun and only one teacher worthy of following Pierre. That person was Marie. Traditions and customs that did not allow for a woman professor needed to be changed.

As the summer wore on, Marie gradually found a new focus—preparing her lectures for the

"Today has seen 'the celebration of a victory for feminism.' If a woman is allowed to teach advanced studies to both sexes, where afterwards will be the pretended superiority of man? I tell you, the time is near when women will become human beings."

"Le Journal," on Marie Curie's first lecture in the Sorbonne, November 6, 1906

Sorbonne. She wanted to do justice to Pierre, to herself, and to the richness of their work together.

Her first lecture, in November 1906, caused a sensation. For the first time ever, a woman was lecturing at the Sorbonne! Long before the lecture began, the hall was packed with scientists, students, society people, curious onlookers, and journalists.

Marie began the lecture at the exact point where Pierre had finished many months before.

The Radium Institute

In the years after Pierre's death, Marie began to formulate a central aim that affected the core of all her efforts. She decided to start a school of radioactivity and to create a team of scientists who would be able to explore the subject even further.

It would be many years before the idea became an actual school. In the meantime, there was much that needed her attention. She continued teaching at the girls' school. At the Sorbonne, she gave the world's first course on radioactivity. She collected all of Pierre's work and published it. Then she did the same with her own research by publishing two massive reference works.

In the lab, she developed a way of measuring the purity and strength of radium preparations. It was important work, especially for therapists who prepared doses for the treatment of cancerous diseases.

In 1911, at the age of forty-four, Marie Curie was awarded a second Nobel Prize, this time in chemistry. She became the first person ever to receive the Nobel Prize twice.

In 1912, the Sorbonne and the famous Pasteur Institute for Medical Research decided to found a Radium Institute in Paris. It would be built on the newly named street, Rue Pierre Curie, and it would be devoted to research in radioactivity and cancer treatment. For almost ten years, cancerous growths

Opposite: After Pierre's death in 1906, Marie worked tirelessly to give other scientists research opportunities. She also isolated radium and polonium as pure salts, for which she earned a second Nobel Prize.

52

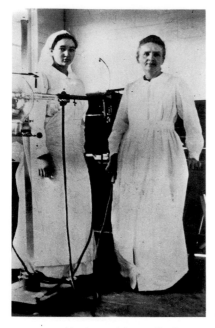

Marie and Irene Curie spent World War I helping to X-ray wounded men. Their work enabled more than a million injured men to receive treatment.

had been treated by radium rays, and recently there had been some spectacular successes.

The building of the Radium Institute began in 1913. Marie personally supervised the garden, choosing the trees and planting the roses. She wanted the institute to be the perfect home for radioactivity long after she was gone! But when the institute was finally completed, World War I had begun. There was no one left to work at the Radium Institute.

Marie's War Effort

Everyone had offered themselves for war work. Marie's instincts told her the war would be a long one and that soldiers would have shattered limbs and terrible wounds from bomb fragments and bullets. The army would need X-ray units to deal with these injuries. There were very few in France and none at the battlefront.

Marie decided that her task would be to set up mobile X-ray units that could travel to the wounded men. She would personally train people to use them. Although she had never worked with X rays, she knew a great deal about them, and she knew she would be able to teach herself how to use an X-ray unit.

Within ten days of her decision, she was touring Paris and asking people for supplies. From wealthy citizens, she obtained money and vehicles. From makers of scientific equipment, university departments, and scientific laboratories, she gradually obtained all the equipment she needed. Then she persuaded car makers to change some of their vehicles into X-ray ambulances. Marie assembled volunteers to work with her from among professors, scientists, and engineers.

By late October of 1914, the first mobile X-ray unit went to the battlefront. It was an ordinary car,

carrying an X-ray machine with a generator that worked off the engine. There were curtains and some screens. There were gloves for the operators to use in order to protect their hands from the rays. In the X-ray unit were Marie, a doctor, two assistants, and a driver-mechanic. One of the assistants was Marie's daughter, Irene, now seventeen.

The first wounded man the X-ray team handled had bullets in his arm, hip, and brain, as well as bomb splinters and fractures throughout his body. The massive injuries shocked Marie and her team. Swiftly they placed the wounded man in front of the machine and searched for the position of all the bullets and fragments of bombs. By the end of the first day, Marie and her team had x-rayed 30 men. By the last two years of the war, more than 1

This picture is of an advanced Red Cross dressing-station during the Battle of Pozieres Ridge in 1916. Marie seemed happy to endure hardship as long as she could help others.

Above: Marie Curie has appeared on stamps from several countries.

Below: A postcard that commemorates the fiftieth anniversary of Marie's death.

million men had passed through Marie's X-ray posts, which consisted of 20 mobile cars and 200 units in the military hospitals.

Marie had trained herself to use the equipment, learned human anatomy, taught herself to drive a car, and even mastered basic car mechanics. She juggled teaching in Paris with assisting at the 400 French and Belgian hospitals at the front. The only thing that kept her from her work were the bouts of her recurring, exhausting, and still-unexplained illness.

She began to think about how radium could help the war effort. By 1915, doctors were using radium to treat scar tissue, arthritis, and other diseases. They had found that the emanation from radium, called radon, was a useful source of curative rays. Marie began to provide tubes of radon for a radium therapy service for all the hospitals.

The Institute Finally Begins

After the war ended, the Radium Institute was able to begin to serve its original purpose. In war-torn France there were few resources. Marie needed equipment and money for the scientific work—and she needed radium.

Since she had first discovered it, the price of radium had climbed. In 1903, Marie had given all her own radium to other scientists. During the war, when it had been used in gunsights and compass cards because of its luminous glow, the price had reached an all-time high.

Marie had made her own radium available for Curietherapy. Now she desperately needed radium for her own research scientists. And Marie, its discoverer, had no money to buy any of it!

Help came from an unexpected source. An American journalist named Marie Meloney invited Marie to go to the United States on a fund-raising tour. Marie shrank from the prospect, but she needed to obtain radium. Reluctantly, she agreed and took her two daughters—Eve, age sixteen, and Irene, age twenty-three—along with her for help and support.

The tour was a huge success. America greeted Marie warmly. Flag-waving crowds cheered her everywhere. Everyone wanted to see the person who had enriched the world with her discovery of radium. Her story captured the public's imagination and in May, 1921, the president of the United States presented Marie Curie with a precious gram of radium.

The adoration and praise was gratifying, but the strain of the journey was too much for Marie. Exhausted and ill, she collapsed and was unable to complete the planned tour. Marie returned to Paris with an understanding of how she could attract money and resources for radium work. As long as she was strong enough, she would make these kinds of tours and work to support the efforts of others. The team Marie gathered at the Institute would, in time, reveal more important secrets regarding radioactivity.

Above: *During her career, Marie Curie received eight major scientific prizes and sixteen medals.*

Below: *A statue of Marya Sklodowska-Curie that stands in front of the Cancer Research Institute in Warsaw.*

Another Curie Triumph

In 1934, Marie's daughter, Irene, was married to Frédéric Joliot, a gifted scientist. They were now attempting to reveal the innermost workings of the atom. In January of 1934, they found that by bombarding some metals with radioactive rays, they could change the metal into a new radioactive substance, not known in nature. They had discovered artificial radioactivity. In 1935, Irene and Frédéric were awarded a Nobel Prize, the third to go to the Curie family.

Meanwhile, Marie's colleague at the Institute, Professor Regaud, continued research on cancer. Between the end of the war and 1935, More than

8,000 patients had been treated. Doctors came to the Institute from all over the world to learn the techniques that had been developed there.

Exposure Takes Its Toll

Marie was precariously close to the end of her lifetime's work. For over a decade now, she had suffered from painful humming in her ears. She was also nearly blind, even though doctors had operated several times on cataracts. These early symptoms of radiation sickness made Marie dizzy and weak, as though she had bad influenza.

Throughout the world, the crippling effects of radium were becoming tragically apparent. In the early 1920s, several workers in a London hospital had died from exposure to radium. Many thousands of laboratory workers all over Europe and America were showing horrifying effects.

One day in May 1934, Marie began to feel particularly ill. She left some work unfinished, telling her staff that she needed to go home to rest and that she would return soon.

She never left her bed again. Suspecting that she

had contracted tuberculosis, Marie was scheduled to go to a sanitorium. Her daughter, Eve, looked after her and the family planned how they would take turns keeping Marie company until she was well again.

On the way to the sanitorium with her temperature soaring, Marie collapsed in Eve's arms. She was in the last stages of radiation sickness, dying from thirty-four years of breathing radioactive air and touching radioactive substances without properly protecting herself.

Science Loses a Pioneer

Marie died on July 4, 1934, at the age of sixty-six. She was buried in the grave where Pierre already lay. Even as family, friends, and the many scientists she had so deeply affected with her work—and her family and friends—gathered around the grave, journalists clambered over the cemetery walls. To them, Marie Curie was public property.

To her family, her children, sisters, and her brother, Marie was the person who had never ceased to inspire them. She had been a source of love and strength since their struggle together in Poland.

Back in 1922, when the scientists of the Academy of Medicine had elected her unanimously to membership, they had said, "We salute in you a great scientist, a great-hearted woman who has lived only through devotion to work and scientific abnegation, a patriot who, in war and peace, has always done more than her duty. Your presence here brings us the moral benefit of your example and the glory of your name. We thank you. We are proud of your presence among us." These words had never before been said to a woman. Thanks to Marie Curie, women everywhere had an opportunity to be honored this way in the future.

· ·

"At the moment when the fame of the two scientists and benefactors was spreading through the world, grief overtook Marie; her husband, her wonderful companion, was taken from her by death in an instant. But in spite of distress and physical illness, she continued alone the work that had been begun with him and brilliantly developed by the science they had created together."

Eve Marie Curie, from
her biography,
"Madame Curie"

· ·

Inside a modern nuclear fuel power station that generates electricity.

Afterword:

Marie Curie's Legacy

Marie Curie left a great deal to the world. Her discovery of radium—and the eventual research that followed—saved and prolonged millions of lives through the treatment of cancer. Her work also led to critical discoveries about the structure of the atom and the eventual development of an atomic bomb and nuclear power.

Marie also raised the standards of science as a whole. She pioneered meticulous methods of observation and data recording, and founded two research institutes where young scientists could be trained in her scientific procedures.

As the first woman doctor of science in Europe, Marie Curie opened up spheres previously barred to women in a profession dominated by men. She was determined to fight for acceptance, and refused to be treated as anything but an equal.

Marie is most famous for her discovery of radium. But her most important scientific discovery came when she established that radiation emerged from inside the atom itself. This simple principle led to the whole development of nuclear physics.

The first inventions that flowed from Marie's discoveries were often fairly frivolous and sometimes dangerous, such as radium face powder, which was marketed in the 1920s. Good innovations followed. Radiation therapy is used to treat cancer, and lasers and radioisotoners are used in various industries to check things, such as the thickness of paper, or to measure the flow of oil through pipelines.

The development of nuclear power may be the most controversial development to arise from Marie Curie's original work. Scientists had suspected there was an almost unbelievable power locked up inside each atom since Albert Einstein (as a result of Curie's

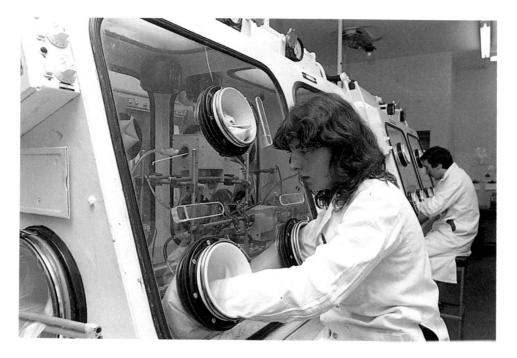

work) suggested this in 1905. By the 1930s, scientists realized that if they could split the atom, this would cause a "chain reaction" that would release an enormous amount of energy. The military application was obvious. On July 15, 1945, the first atomic bomb was tested in New Mexico. Millions of dollars were poured into research for other uses of atomic power. A nuclear submarine, the USS Nautilus, was launched in 1954. The first civilian nuclear power station was commissioned in the USSR in the same year.

Marie Curie dedicated her life to science out of a profound belief that the benefits of nuclear energy far outweighed the dangers. This was Marie's humanitarian contribution. Today, the biggest challenge that remains is to make the correct use of the technology that Marie Curie inspired.

Marie Curie pioneered the field of scientific research for women, and made it possible for women to advance in all areas of scientific investigation.

. . . .

"Marie Curie is, of all celebrated beings, the one whom fame has not corrupted."

Albert Einstein

. . . .

Important Dates

1867	**November 7:** Marya Sklodowska born in Warsaw, Poland.
1876	Marya's sister, Sofia, dies of typhus fever.
1878	Marya's mother dies of tuberculosis; Marya is 10.
1883	Marya finishes school, and then spends a year in the country.
1884	Returns to Warsaw and joins "The Floating University."
1886	Starts work as a governess, aged eighteen.
1891	Marya, aged twenty-three, leaves for Paris to study at the Sorbonne.
1893	Heads her class in obtaining her Physics degree.
1894	Meets Pierre Curie. She obtains a second degree in Mathematics.
1895	**July 26:** Marries Pierre Curie in a civil ceremony. **November 8:** Wilhelm Roentgen, a German physicist, discovers X rays.
1896	**February 28:** Becquerel, a French physicist, discovers radioactivity.
1897	**September 12:** Birth of Irene. Marie's research into radioactivity starts.
1898	**April 12:** Marie's first paper presented to the Academie des Sciences. **June 6:** Marie isolates polonium. **December:** Marie isolates radium.
1902	Marie distills the first pure radium.
1903	Marie receives her doctorate for her work on radium. With Henri Becquerel, the Curies receive the Nobel Prize for Physics.
1904	**December:** Birth of Eve.
1906	**April 19:** Pierre Curie is killed by a horse-drawn cart. **November:** Marie is the first woman ever to lecture at the Sorbonne.
1911	**January 23:** Marie is awarded the Nobel Prize for Chemistry.
1912	Marie named as Director of the Radium Institute in Paris.
1914	The Radium Institute is finished on July 3; on August 4 war is declared.
1914-18	Marie organizes mobile X-ray units for the war and trains 150 operators.
1921	**May 20:** U.S. President Harding presents one gram of radium to Marie.
1926	Irene Curie marries Frédéric Joliot, a French physicist.
1934	Irene and Frédéric discover artificial radioactivity. **July 4:** Marie dies of radiation poisoning.
1935	Irene and Frédéric receive the Nobel Prize for Physics.
1937	Eve's biography of her mother, *Madame Curie*, published.
1945	The first atom bomb is exploded at Alamagordo; the atomic age begins.

For More Information

Books

Fisher, Leonard. *Marie Curie.* New York, NY: Simon & Schuster, 1994.

Parker, Steve. *Marie Curie and Radium* (Scientific Discoveries Series). New York, NY: Chelsea House, 1995.

Web Site

Marie Curie—Find out more about this famous physicist and other great scientists who changed the world-www.lucidcafe.com/lucidcafe/library/95nov/curie.html

Glossary

Actinium: A radioactive metallic element, a decay produce of uranium. Its atomic number is 89.

Alpha rays: Positively charged helium nuclei that are absorbed by a sheet of paper or thin metal foil. Air is ionized considerably when alpha particles are passed through, but they have a range of only a few centimeters.

Atom: The smallest quantity of an element that can take part in a chemical reaction. Atoms are composed of neutrons and protons in a nucleus surrounded by electrons.

Atomic number: The number of protons in the nucleus of an atom of an element.

Beta rays: Negatively-charged electrons that have a greater penetrating power than alpha rays. Their range in air is also greater than alpha particles, but when passed through air, their ionization is relatively smaller.

Curietherapy or Radiation therapy: The treatment of disease, particularly cancer, by radiation.

Distilling: A chemical process that purifies a liquid by boiling it and condensing the resulting gas.

Elements: The basic substances of the world. There are 113 elements, of which 90 are natural. The rest have been manufactured.

Emanation: A radioactive gas produced by the disintegration of a radioactive substance.

Filtering: A physical process that removes solids from a liquid by letting it soak through a porous substance.

Gamma rays: Similar to X rays, but of a shorter wavelength. They have much less ionizing power, but are able to penetrate large thicknesses of metals.

Half life: The time taken for half the atoms in a radioactive material to decay. This can be from less than a second to 4,510 million years (for Uranium 238's alpha radiation).

Isotope: Two or more forms of the same element, with a different number of neutrons in the nucleus. Radioisotopes emit radiation.

Nobel Prize: Founded by Alfred Nobel (1833-96) who invented dynamite. First awarded in 1901 for Physics, Chemistry, Medicine, Literature, and Peace.

Pitchblende: An ore often found with silver: the principal source of uranium and radium.

Polonium: A very rare radioactive element; its atomic number is 84.

Radiation Sickness: Caused by over-exposure to alpha, beta, gamma, or X rays. First symptoms include vomiting, diarrhea, and hair loss.

Radioactivity: The emission of radiant energy from a material as alpha, beta, or gamma rays as the nuclei of the atoms break up.

Radium: A highly radioactive luminous element found mostly in pitchblende and other uranium-bearing ores. Its atomic number is 88.

Sanitorium: Residential establishment where the chronically sick are treated.

Thorium: A soft radioactive metallic element; Marie Curie started by researching it. Its atomic number is 90.

uranium: A radioactive metallic element, found in pitchblende and other ores. Its atomic number is 92.

X rays: Discovered by Wilhelm Roentgen (1845-1923) in 1895. Their wavelengths lie between ultraviolet light and gamma rays.

Index